"Sustainability informs every decision[...] every decision we make better. Dan ([...] get you on the road to how to rethin[...]

GW00494967

DANIEL T. HENDRIX, CHAIRMAN AND CHIEF EX[...]

"CSR is dead. Corporate Sustainability is finally here and it's asking a lot more of companies and their brands than CSR ever did. For those executives still not persuaded that all this 'sustainability stuff' is for them, this book is just great."

JONATHON PORRITT, FOUNDER DIRECTOR—FORUM FOR THE FUTURE

"Dan Gray may not be Dan Brown, but his 55-minute guide is a real page-turner."

JOHN ELKINGTON, CO-FOUNDER—VOLANS VENTURES

"As Dan Gray argues, more and more companies are seeing how sustainability must be part of core business, not simply a token add-on. This short, direct and engaging book will help anyone interested in this debate to get their head around key concepts and challenges."

MATTHEW TAYLOR, CHIEF EXECUTIVE, RSA

"Dan Gray makes a powerful, well-argued case for the need to build sustainable brands that fulfil their contract with the environment as well as with customers. It's the way forward, and this book shows us how."

JEREMY MOON, FOUNDER AND CHIEF EXECUTIVE—ICEBREAKER CLOTHING

"This is a great user manual for those coming to terms with the realisation that old fashioned corporate responsibility should be confined to the dustbin of history."

TONY MANWARING, CHIEF EXECUTIVE—TOMORROW'S COMPANY

"'Baked in' sustainability is a completely different proposition to 'bolt-on' CSR. For business leaders who have yet to grasp the difference—and the enormous opportunities that lay within—the carefully woven arguments in this book are a great place to start."

TRISTAN LLOYD-BAKER, COMMERCIAL DIRECTOR—AEROTHERMAL

"A fiendishly handy primer on turning sustainability into a source of brand and competitive advantage. All you need to know to get the big idea in less than an hour."

MATT GITSHAM, DIRECTOR—ASHRIDGE CENTRE FOR BUSINESS AND SUSTAINABILITY

"Dan Gray is doing something very important for the evolution of the sustainability debate in business. Cutting through the swathes of commentary that rely on a more technical case, he speaks directly and persuasively to those responsible for motivating employees, customers and consumers."

GUY CHAMPNISS, ADVISOR TO HAVAS AND THE WORLD BUSINESS COUNCIL FOR SUSTAINABLE DEVELOPMENT, AND AUTHOR OF **BRAND VALUED**

"A clear, concise and insightful summary of where Corporate Responsibility and sustainability is at. There isn't a marketer in Britain who wouldn't gain from giving an hour of their time to read and reflect on its contents."

GILES GIBBONS, FOUNDER AND CHIEF EXECUTIVE—GOOD BUSINESS

"A very skillfully crafted think-piece. Dan Gray's argument that sustainability equals longevity is brilliantly thought-provoking."

ROBERT JONES, HEAD OF NEW THINKING—WOLFF OLINS

"A sensitive interpretation of the best contemporary business thinking and a compelling case for a systems-led approach to value creation. Dan Gray provokes the kind of inquiry that 21st century managers must make to innovate and succeed for the long term."

RICHARD EISERMANN, FORMER DIRECTOR OF DESIGN AND INNOVATION—THE DESIGN COUNCIL

"Dan's book is a pleasure to read. Easy to devour in under an hour, it'll reward you with some great insights into the subtleties of building a sustainable brand. Tickling your mind, making you think and bringing a smile, it's definitely a book to keep close to hand."

MORAG HUTCHEON, DESIGN DIRECTOR—QUADRO DESIGN ASSOCIATES, AND BRITISH FEMALE INVENTOR OF THE YEAR 2006

"You attract more flies with honey than with vinegar, as my grandmother used to say. That's what I like about this book, and why I use it prominently in one of my courses. Not just for sustainable neophytes, it offers refreshing perspectives for the grizzled veteran too."

PHIL HAMLETT, GRADUATE DIRECTOR—ACADEMY OF ART UNIVERSITY, AND AMBASSADOR—THE LIVING PRINCIPLES

LIVE LONG AND PROSPER

THE 55-MINUTE GUIDE TO
BUILDING SUSTAINABLE BRANDS
BY **DAN GRAY**

CHAIN OF CUSTODY
ALL BOOKS IN THE 55-MINUTE GUIDE SERIES ARE 'PRINT ON DEMAND' (POD), A
MODEL OFFERING SIGNIFICANT ENVIRONMENTAL ADVANTAGES OVER TRADITIONAL
OFFSET PRINTING. THE PRINTER OF THIS BOOK, LIGHTNING SOURCE®, IS CHAIN OF
CUSTODY (COC) CERTIFIED BY THE FOREST STEWARDSHIP COUNCIL™ (FSC®), THE
PROGRAMME FOR THE ENDORSEMENT OF FOREST CERTIFICATION™ (PEFC™) AND
THE SUSTAINABLE FORESTRY INITIATIVE® (SFI®), ENSURING THE INTEGRITY OF THE
PAPER SUPPLY CHAIN AND THAT THE PAPER USED IN PRINTING THIS BOOK IS FROM
RESPONSIBLY MANAGED FORESTS.

FIRST PUBLISHED IN 2010 BY
VERB PUBLISHING LTD
THE COW SHED, HYDE HALL FARM,
BUCKLAND, HERTS SG9 0RU,
UNITED KINGDOM

ISBN 978-0-9564672-9-4

WHAT'S INSIDE

1. PREFACE

So, what's changed since the first edition of this book was published two years ago? The short answer, paradoxically, is both everything and nothing.

Slightly depressingly, what hasn't changed is the vast majority of companies' understanding of what it really means to be sustainable.

The ones who get the concepts and arguments laid out in this book have got it for a long time already. These include not only newer kids on the block, like the brilliant Icebreaker in New Zealand, for whom sustainability is the very inspiration behind their highly successful performance clothing business. They also comprise long-established corporations like Interface—the world's largest manufacturer of modular carpet—and British retail icon, Marks & Spencer, who have long since understood the major discontinuity represented by the combined impacts of population growth, diminishing resources, climate change and increased public scrutiny.

They have recognised the changing frame conditions within which business is now operating and that their long-term prosperity depends on nothing less than the redesign of core business strategy and operations.

Meanwhile, by and large, those who didn't get it before recession struck still don't get it now. Indeed, if anything, all recession has done is to entrench short-term thinking.

And yet...

Everywhere I look, MOMENTUM IS GROWING. Sustainability is no longer the exclusive realm of hair-shirted environmentalists and pie-in-the-sky idealists.

The idea that CREATING SHARED VALUE might be the great competitive advantage of the 21st century—that, to achieve lasting and meaningful success, business must reconnect strategy to a sense of SOCIAL PROGRESS—is rapidly gaining currency, even in the hallowed corridors of Harvard Business School and other temples of traditional, left-brained management thinking.

When the doyen of competitive strategy, Michael Porter, starts proselytising about a more constructive form of capitalism, you know it's time to pull on your track shoes. The kind of stuff that people like Paul Hawken, Ray C. Anderson and Jonathon Porritt have been talking and writing about for ages has finally hit the mainstream!

And for every poster-child of old-world CSR to have come an almighty cropper in recent times (not least BP, whose 'Beyond Petroleum' greenwash has come back to bite them royally on the bum in the wake of the Deepwater Horizon disaster in the Gulf of Mexico), there's a story of another major corporation embracing new-world sustainability.

Consider the launch in 2011 of Unilever's Sustainable Living Plan, for example, explicitly framed by CEO, Paul Polman, "not as a project to celebrate, but a NEW BUSINESS MODEL TO IMPLEMENT," based on the fundamental understanding that materially addressing sustainability not only offers opportunities to save costs, but is also a critical engine of INNOVATION AND BRAND EQUITY.

In short, then, the case for building sustainable brands—and for a book that gives sympaticos and sceptics alike a quick and easy way of getting to grips with the big idea and how to action it—has never been stronger.

Don't worry. Despite the inclusion of new ideas culled from my blog—plus some older ones, re-examined and expanded upon in light of putting them into practice with clients—I promise you'll still be able to read this book from cover to cover in under an hour.

I hope you enjoy it.

Live long and prosper!

On every facing page you'll find a summary of core thoughts and ideas. Try adding them to presentations or the bottom of your emails and see if you can start a conversation.

2. INTRODUCTION

WHAT THIS BOOK'S ABOUT

A lot of people are talking about sustainability these days. Still more talk about brands. Yet very few people truly understand either. This book is inspired by the likes of Marty Neumeier (**THE BRAND GAP, ZAG** and **THE DESIGNFUL COMPANY**) and Edward de Bono (**SIMPLICITY**). It isn't meant to be an all-singing, all-dancing how-to guide, full of detailed case studies and examples. It's a primer—a quick and dirty tour around the massively complex (and yet fundamentally simple) worlds of brand, design and sustainability, and how they are converging.

My aims? First, to give very busy people a book they can read in less than an hour. Second, to focus on the really important insights, so you know enough to be dangerous, without having to wade through reams of information. Third, to get you thinking and talking in a COMPLETELY DIFFERENT LANGUAGE about sustainability—less about moral imperatives and more about HARD BUSINESS LOGIC and the value to be derived from adopting more sustainable strategies. In short, it's about the case for building sustainable brands.

The goal of this book is simple—to give you some powerful ideas that will help you to answer the questions that really matter when it comes to sustainability.

It's written primarily for current and aspiring CEOs, and other senior executives in their organisations and the consultancies that support them—people who not only have an interest in how sustainability is likely to shape their business in the future, but who also have the influence and authority to actually DO SOMETHING ABOUT IT. Hopefully, by the end of it, you'll at least have a few ideas to get you started on tackling what are some pretty big questions:

→ What does sustainability look like in my (client's) organisation?

→ Why is that critical to long-term brand and business success?

→ How can I turn sustainability into a meaningful source of brand and competitive advantage?

HOW IT'S STRUCTURED

First, we'll look at what it means to be 'sustainable'. With so many different terms in circulation—Corporate Responsibility, Corporate Social Responsibility (CSR), Corporate Citizenship etc.—and wildly differing approaches to the management of ethical and ecological concerns, it's hardly surprising that business, and society at large, often finds it hard to get a

As we go along, we'll pluck out seven principles for building sustainable brands. You'll also find them listed on page 98. You can skip ahead for a better indication of what this book's about. Or you can wait until you reach them and they'll provide you with a handy summary.

grip on what sustainability REALLY MEANS. This section cuts through the crap to get to the heart of what it should be about (regardless of what you call it) and why it's critical to long-term brand and business success.

Second, we'll explore what it means to be a sustainable brand in the broadest sense of having the capacity to survive and prosper in the long-term. Amongst other things, we'll look at why companies don't actually own their brands and what that means for their search for the authentic voice.

Third, we'll delve much more deeply into what it means to be a sustainable brand in the more popular sense of making a positive contribution to society and the environment. We'll look at something called the CR CONTINUUM—probably the simplest way to illustrate how and when organisations can build genuine brand and competitive advantage through action on sustainability.

As we go along, we'll pluck out SEVEN PRINCIPLES for building a sustainable brand and establishing a meaningful claim to differentiation. (And, in case you miss them, they'll be summarised in a handy set of take-home lessons at the end of the book.)

When you hear the word sustainability, don't think green, think longevity. It's about the capacity to survive and prosper over generations.

3. WHAT IS SUSTAINABILITY?

As man's role in climate change has become ever clearer, so sustainability has become largely synonymous with environmental concerns—essentially, how can we continue to grow and develop as a society, without causing irreparable harm to our ecosystem?

It's also a term that has tended to be used interchangeably with the many others—CR, CSR, Corporate Citizenship etc.— that organisations use to denote activities and investments designed to illustrate their status as responsible enterprises.

Frankly, both usages get in the way of a proper and useful understanding of what it means to be sustainable. In its original and broadest sense, sustainability is simply about longevity—THE CAPACITY TO SURVIVE AND PROSPER OVER GENERATIONS. In business, that naturally includes dimensions of ethical behaviour (you're not going to do very well if your stakeholders don't trust you) and environmental stewardship (likewise, you're not going to be able operate efficiently if you're reliant on ever scarcer and more expensive natural resources), but it's about much more than that.

Asking how a business is socially or environmentally responsible and how it is sustainable should be two completely

Sustainability is a perspective on brand and business strategy that inextricably links long-term success with serving a higher social purpose.

different questions. The latter is infinitely broader in scope, essentially: WHY WILL YOU STILL BE IN BUSINESS IN 50 YEARS' TIME?

Understanding sustainability in these terms makes it much easier to engage with sceptical business leaders, because it takes sustainability out of the realm of the sandal-wearing, tree-hugging, save-the-whale brigade and into the realm of what they really care about—RUNNING A SUCCESSFUL BUSINESS. What's more, it fosters a completely different mindset about how to tackle the issue. Sustainability ceases to be seen as a separate agenda, and is instead positioned as AN INTEGRAL PART OF BUSINESS STRATEGY AND OPERATIONS.

And that's how it should be seen. Ultimately, sustainability is not a discrete function, programme or initiative. It's a CULTURAL THING—a fundamental belief and way of thinking that encourages us to consider the long-term implications of our actions. (If you're fond of soundbites, think of it this way: CR WITHOUT HR IS JUST PR.)

There are many definitions of sustainability—most of them pretty lame. The one that forms the core of this book is simple and it reads as follows: sustainability is a PERSPECTIVE ON BRAND AND BUSINESS STRATEGY that inextricably links long-term success with SERVING A HIGHER SOCIAL PURPOSE.

If people still need to hear the business case for sustainability, then they haven't read enough. It's a no-brainer.

4. THE BUSINESS CASE FOR SUSTAINABILITY

In some ways, I wonder why I even feel compelled to write this section. Unfortunately, coming from a background in brand and engagement, I've been through this all before—obstinate business leaders demanding evidence for something that was always blindingly obvious (well-motivated people work harder and deliver better service to customers, leading to improved business performance—go figure!).

The fact of the matter (as will hopefully become abundantly clear) is that sustainability ought to be a no-brainer. Doing nothing is no longer an option if you still want to be a successful business in fifty years' time.

If it's in-depth analysis you want, then take a look at Chapter 14 of CAPITALISM AS IF THE WORLD MATTERS by Jonathon Porritt. If you're happy to make do with the high-level overview then, broadly speaking, the business benefits fall into three main categories:

→ COST AND RISK REDUCTION – the most obvious benefits are derived from savings to the bottom line and better risk management, through things like waste reduction and energy efficiency.

Sustainability = £££ (whichever way you look at it).

→ REPUTATION AND LEGITIMACY – further obvious benefits range from maintaining the so-called LICENCE TO OPERATE to acting as an important tool for attracting customers, investors and top talent.

→ INNOVATION AND GROWTH TRAJECTORY – less obvious, but by far the most profound, sustainability's increasing significance suggests it as a key avenue for DISRUPTIVE INNOVATION, leading to more radical, long-term differentiation.

In short, there's something for everyone. However you derive competitive advantage as a business—be it through operational excellence, product leadership or customer intimacy—there's a case for integrating sustainable thinking in your organisation.

EXPLODING THE MYTH OF EITHER/OR

I may say that the business case is a no-brainer, but that's only really true if you've already made the leap in understanding from sustainability as something tangential to core business to something that is an integral part of it.

Sustainability and profitability aren't mutually exclusive. Companies like Interface provide an undeniable example that we can have both.

The point about sustainability as an increasingly significant driver of innovation and growth is crucial, because it gives the lie to the myth that the pursuit of sustainability and the pursuit of profit are mutually exclusive. Provided you're smart about it, there's NO REASON YOU CAN'T HAVE BOTH, as proven by companies like Interface.

Its profits have MORE THAN DOUBLED as a result of its Mission Zero strategy to completely eliminate any negative impact on the environment by 2020—a combination of efficiency savings, the galvanising effect on employees, a well-spring of new product and process innovations, and the generation of a level of goodwill that no amount of fancy marketing could ever buy.

It explodes the myth of either/or, showing that it is eminently possible to be both sustainable AND profitable— indeed to become MORE PROFITABLE by adopting more sustainable strategies. Mission Zero also provides a great example of what Jim Collins and Jerry Porras would call a Big Hairy Audacious Goal (or BHAG). In fact, take a look at the Interface story and you'll find a great deal of crossover with these and other themes from their seminal book, **BUILT TO LAST**, which examines the reasons behind the enduring success of 18 companies over more than a century,

Business doesn't exist to make a profit, it makes a profit to exist. Discuss.

and challenges a number of widely held assumptions about running a successful business.

When it comes to the broader definition of sustainability as longevity, it's a powerful handbook and it provides possibly the most powerful business case of all.

Why should companies aim for longevity? Why should they build for the long-term, even in a time of downturn? Why should they put an enduring purpose and values ahead of short-term profit maximisation?

The answer's simple—BECAUSE IT PAYS.

On average, a dollar invested in 1926 in one of the successful comparison companies featured in the book would have grown to $995 by 1991, or twice the rate of return of the general market. Had that dollar been invested in one of the built to last companies, that figure would have been $6,356, the equivalent of 15 times the general market return (some difference, you have to agree).

Those businesses that have stood the test of time have done so because, whilst they always set out to make money, it was never their sole objective. In short, counter-intuitive though it may seem, the single-minded pursuit of profit would appear to produce LESS OF IT than if it is seen as the by-product of serving A HIGHER PURPOSE.

Old-world CSR is about giving something back. It says, "We contribute to society because we are successful."

New-world sustainability is about creating shared value. It says, "We are successful because we contribute to society."

5. CHANGING TIMES

OLD-WORLD CSR VS. NEW-WORLD SUSTAINABILITY

Stories like that of Interface signal a quantum shift in strategy and practice. It's as fundamental as the shift from Web 1.0 to Web 2.0, which is a handy analogy to summarise the differences.

Old-world CSR—what you might refer to as CR 1.0—is essentially about 'CR as PR'. It's a self-contained box for all the good stuff—a tactical bolt-on to business as usual, designed to protect and enhance corporate reputation. Communications are dominated by talk of ethics and values, and by examples of corporate philanthropy, in an effort to persuade naysayers that they're really a kind and considerate bunch. It's what's still practised by the vast majority of organisations today and—as designer, Bruce Mau, so memorably describes it in Warren Berger's excellent book, GLIMMER—it tends to make most organisations' efforts look like, "an island of intelligence in a sea of stupidity."

New-world sustainability—CR 2.0—adopts a radically different focus. Here, sustainability is fully integrated into organisational culture—A FUNDAMENTAL DESIGN VALUE, designed to challenge and transform existing practices and

The irony is that those who take action on sustainability purely in order to protect and enhance their reputation may end up doing their brands more harm than good.

shape corporate strategy. Communications are dominated by talk of VALUE CREATION, and by examples of how sustainable thinking has led to major product and process innovations, in an effort to demonstrate to naysayers that businesses can actually do extremely well by doing good. It's understood and practised by very few organisations, and best encapsulated by the late, great Ray C. Anderson (founder and chairman of Interface) as, "a better way to bigger, more legitimate profits."

In short, the language—and, more importantly, the value proposition—has changed dramatically and, where thought leaders go, everyone else will eventually be bound to follow. The business case has shifted emphasis and organisations stuck in the world of CR 1.0 risk being left behind.

Indeed, the irony is that those who take action on sustainability purely in order to protect and enhance their reputation may end up doing their brands more harm than good. (HOLD THAT THOUGHT—we'll talk about it more later.)

THE IMPACT OF RECESSION

"Can CR survive the recession?" has become a popular question over the last couple of years. It's also a misguided one. The case for practising business more sustainably doesn't collapse, simply because of challenging times.

Car buyers are now poring over fuel economy figures and CO_2 emissions as intensely as they used to compare 0-60 times.

The only reason this question even gets asked is because so many people still think in terms of CR as PR. In that guise, it's dead, and good riddance to it!

Far from sounding the death knell, recession actually raises the stakes. Hot on the heels of corporate scandals like Enron and WorldCom, the global financial crisis—likewise seen as the result of excessive corporate greed—has only led to people shining an even brighter light on organisations' ethical credentials.

In any event, reframe the question and it should be clear that sustainability makes more sense now than ever. Can good corporate governance survive a recession? Can trusted relationships with employees, customers and suppliers survive a recession? Can energy efficiency survive a recession? OF COURSE THEY CAN.

What's more, there are signs that this recession (depression?) is providing a much-needed kick up the backside for us to adopt more sustainable behaviours. Just look at the motor industry's charge to manufacture electric vehicles— everything from the Nissan Leaf to the Tesla supercar—and customers now poring over fuel economy figures and CO_2 emissions with the same fervour as used to be devoted to comparing 0-60 times.

How long will businesses survive and prosper with unsustainable business models? Former M&S boss, Sir Stuart Rose, reckons 20 years max.

Against this sort of backdrop, any organisation that pulls back from its sustainability investments now is effectively announcing to the world that they were opportunistic and for short-term gain—firmly stuck in the world of CR 1.0—rather than part of a considered, long-term strategy. In so doing, they'll be driving the final nail into the coffin of credibility.

What's more, their steadfast adherence to an exclusively left-brained, 20th century, industrial-age paradigm might just be dooming them to failure. Not immediately perhaps, but within the next 20 years. At least that's what Sir Stuart Rose predicted in his speech as outgoing chairman of Marks & Spencer in 2010, and I happen to agree with him!

FOR-PURPOSE TRUMPS FOR-PROFIT?

Plenty of other people agree too. Whether it's the passionate polemics of Umair Haque or the more sober analyses of sustainability gurus like John Elkington, economists like David Korten, or leading authorities on corporate strategy like Gary Hamel and Roger Martin, a broad consensus is very definitely forming that we're living at the dawn of a NEW NORMAL—something much more profound than mere recession.

The rules of the game have changed. Purpose maximisation, not profit maximisation might just be the new maxim for 21st century business.

It's a major DISCONTINUITY—one to cause us to rethink not only how businesses create value, but WHAT CONSTITUTES VALUE IN THE FIRST PLACE.

You could call it a perfect storm—the combined force of population growth, diminishing resources, climate change and increased public scrutiny all striking at the same time. But that's not all. You also have the potentially seismic combination of the ascent of the Millennials plus—just as importantly—an entire generation of baby-boomers turning sixty and wondering just what kind of legacy they're leaving behind them (Gates Foundation, anyone?).

It all amounts to a very different set of assumptions, and signs are already emerging that PURPOSE MAXIMISATION, rather than profit maximisation might just be the maxim for 21st century business.

Take the new forms of incorporation like the 'low profit limited liability corporation' (L3C for short) and the 'B-corporation' cropping up in the US—ones that put LONG-TERM VALUE AND SOCIAL IMPACT above short-term economic gain. Take Jack Welch, poster boy for the maximising shareholder value crowd, turning round and dubbing it "THE DUMBEST IDEA IN THE WORLD". Take Harvard and McKinsey jointly launching THE LONG-TERM CAPITALISM

When Harvard and McKinsey jointly launch a competition to accelerate the reinvention of capitalism as a force for good in society, you know you've reached a tipping point!

CHALLENGE—a competition to find examples that can accelerate the reinvention of capitalism as a force for good in the 21st century. Take these examples—and the many more that exist—and it's hard not to think that we've reached a tipping point.

WHY LOOK THROUGH THE LENS OF BRAND?

Curly: You know what the secret of life is?

Mitch: No, what?

Curly: This.

Mitch: Your finger?

Curly: One thing. Just one thing. You stick to that and everything else don't mean shit.

Mitch: That's great, but what's the one thing?

Curly: That's what you've got to figure out.

Now, I'm not normally one for finding deep philosophical meaning in movies or song lyrics, but these lines from an old comedy favourite—CITY SLICKERS—seem rather apt. From Umair Haque's rallying call for business to create THICKER VALUE to my fellow 55-minute guide and CommScrum co-conspirator Mike Klein's musings on an AGE OF INTENT, one thing is for sure—PURPOSE MATTERS LIKE NEVER BEFORE.

The consequences of thin value—of profit decoupled from the people and resources impacted by its generation—have been exposed like never before in our lifetime.

Charles Handy said it best in 2002 in what is probably my favourite Harvard Business Review article of all time—one that goes by the fiendishly simple title of **WHAT'S A BUSINESS FOR?** In it, he makes the profound observation that most shareholders these days are little more than gamblers, and that to turn their needs into your sole raison d'être is to be guilty of confusing a necessary condition for a sufficient one.

"The purpose of a business," he concludes, "is not to make a profit, full stop. It is to make a profit SO THAT THE BUSINESS CAN DO SOMETHING MORE OR BETTER. That 'something' becomes the real justification for the business' existence." Whilst that may have been said before, in the wake of the global financial crisis and other catastrophes, like the BP oil spill in the Gulf of Mexico, it has a new resonance.

The consequences of THIN VALUE—of profit decoupled from the people and resources impacted by its generation—have been exposed like never before in our lifetime. It's time for businesses to put the organisational WHY—Curly's one thing—ahead of the who, the what and the how. Why do you exist? What purpose do you serve? If you ceased to exist tomorrow, why should anyone miss you? Now, some might call that a MISSION. Mike labels it INTENT. Me? I call it a BRAND, which leads us rather neatly into the next chapter...

Your brand isn't what you say it is. It's what they say it is, and everything you do has the power either to enhance or erode it.

6. BUILDING SUSTAINABLE BRANDS

BRAND 101

Let's start with the basics...

Simply put, a brand is a promise—a proxy for an actual or expected experience. It artfully communicates your BIG IDEA—the essence of what's different and special about your organisation, products and services.

At least, that's the view you'll get from a lot of brand managers and, whilst they're not wrong, they're not entirely right either. That's because what you say your brand is doesn't really count. What matters is what THEY SAY IT IS—your customers, employees, investors and other key stakeholders.

Ultimately, brand is a set of TACIT ASSUMPTIONS and PRECONSCIOUS BELIEFS held by other people about your organisation, what it does and how it does it—YOUR REPUTATION.

It doesn't exist in isolation. It's a reflection of all the tangible and intangible assets that make up your business. EVERYTHING YOU SAY AND DO has the potential either to enhance or erode it.

It only exists in other people's minds, so there's really no such thing as brand management (how can you manage what's in someone else's head?). The best you can do is

To survive and prosper in the long-term, a brand must be distinctive and memorable but—above all—it must be true.

steer people's perceptions by ensuring that the gap between what you promise and what they experience is as small as humanly possible.

Remembering that sustainability, in its broadest sense, is about longevity, all this leads to the FIRST PRINCIPLE for building sustainable brands. For a brand to survive and prosper over the long-term, it must be distinctive and memorable but—above all—IT MUST BE TRUE.

THE QUEST FOR AUTHENTICITY

Authenticity is by no means a new word in the world of brand and business communications, but it's certainly cropping up more and more these days (not surprising really when you consider the events of the last few years).

The pendulum is inevitably swinging back towards brands built on substance, rather than spin. That used to mean substance at the micro-level, emphasising the features and benefits of a particular product or service. But in a world where brands now represent IDENTITY—a statement about who we are and how we want to be seen—it means something much bigger.

It means showing people WHAT YOU STAND FOR.

Authenticity and competitive advantage rest on the proper branding of internal culture—a clear and transparent demonstration of what you stand for.

People don't want to be sold to. They care far less about features and benefits than they do about what the decision to buy from—or work for—a given organisation says about them. They want to buy—and buy into—a big idea that reinforces their sense of self.

Remembering that your brand is what they say it is, AUTHENTICITY IS IMPOSSIBLE WITHOUT TRANSPARENCY. The measure is the extent to which a brand's core purpose is demonstrably enshrined in the way that product, service or company performs. Particularly for corporate and service brands, this means that authenticity and competitive advantage rest increasingly on the PROPER BRANDING OF INTERNAL CULTURE.

If you're familiar with UK retailer, John Lewis, you'll know the sort of thing I mean. The proof of its brand essence —that sense of British fair play that underpins its customer promise of "Never knowingly undersold"—is to be found first and foremost in the organisation's foundation as a partnership, co-owned by each and every person who works there. Among other things, that's a credo that saw £194.5m in bonuses in 2011 distributed evenly among all 'partners' at the rate of 18% of salary. Chairman Charlie Mayfield's reward for presiding over a double-digit increase in profits? LESS THAN £200K. (Bank bosses, watch and learn!)

Building an authentic value proposition takes a lot more than brand specialism. Brands are increasingly a reflection of entire business models, not just products and services.

A NEW AGE OF THE POLYMATH?

The challenge of creating a truly authentic brand proposition just got a whole lot bigger. If authentic brands are those that embody the internal culture of an organisation—increasingly a reflection of ENTIRE BUSINESS MODELS, not just products and services—then brand stewards need to broaden their outlook.

Just as authenticity is impossible without transparency, SO TRANSPARENCY IS IMPOSSIBLE WITHOUT SIMPLICITY. Trouble is, business is a complex system.

Making sense of that complexity and generating compelling brand insights increasingly requires knowledge of ALL ASPECTS of business management in order to get under the skin of an organisation as a whole, to uncover what is truly valuable about its services, strategy and culture, and to arrive at a brand essence that can be embraced and operationalised by ALL PARTS of the business.

Not only that, it also requires BROAD-BANDWIDTH THINKING to truly understand the impact of the seismic shifts taking place all around us—the changing set of frame conditions in which business is now operating, as highlighted in chapter 5—and to reimagine these contextual forces, not as constraints, but as OPPORTUNITIES TO RECONNECT with disillusioned customers and employees.

Deep functional specialism is ill-equipped to deal with complexity. An age of discontinuity demands interdisciplinary approaches to strategy and communication.

As UK design legend Richard Seymour argues with characteristic irreverence in **THE FUTURE OF THE FUTURE**, "This is Renaissance 2. And this time, it's personal!" And just like the 16th century version, the polymaths' prowess as integrative thinkers and sense-makers will be right to the fore as we seek to solve WICKED PROBLEMS like sustainability.

Back to Curly's 'one thing' again, what should be clear is that you're unlikely to reach a deeply resonant answer to what that is—an analogue to Google's "organize the world's information", or Interface's "not one fresh drop of new oil"—if you come at it from the inch-wide, mile-deep perspective of the functional expert. You need to be part management consultant, part futurologist, part designer, part behavioural economist, part occupational psychologist, part operations manager, part HR professional, part strategic marketer, part media relations expert, even part accountant. Brand specialism is no longer enough, no matter how strategically you claim to practise.

In summary, the SECOND PRINCIPLE for building sustainable brands states that sustainability is too pervasive to be managed along narrow, functional lines. It is the responsibility of everyone in the organisation and requires an INTERDISCIPLINARY APPROACH to strategy and communication.

CR as PR is dead. Businesses need to start thinking much more strategically about the actions they take in the name of sustainability.

MATERIALITY IS KING

Building a credible commitment to sustainability—in its popular sense of ethical behaviour and making a positive contribution to society and the environment—is an equally challenging task.

In a world of sceptical and savvy consumers, old school corporate philanthropy just doesn't cut it any more. People are looking for something more—evidence that organisations are actually INTERROGATING AND CHANGING THE WAY THEY OPERATE, not just conducting business as usual, then seeking to soften the blow. (That way lie accusations of greenwashing, and rightly so.)

It means that businesses need to think much more strategically about the actions they take in the name of sustainability. A good place to start is to follow the principles of awareness, responsiveness and materiality:

→ AWARENESS – Knowing what's happening. Show people that you truly understand how what you do impacts on society and the environment—for better and for worse.

Sustainability isn't about PR, it's about culture. (Hmm... did I say that already?!)

→   RESPONSIVENESS – Knowing what to do about it. Manage those issues transparently, enabling both friends and critics to see how that's shaped your strategic priorities.

→   MATERIALITY – Knowing what's important. Prioritise action on the issues that really matter to the business and its stakeholders.

All three are important, but MATERIALITY IS KING. Authenticity ultimately stems from the ability to see a clear line of sight between impact and action. Rather than just a bunch of random philanthropic investments, activities are focused on issues that are DIRECTLY RELEVANT TO—and MOST IMPACTED BY— your business' strategy and operations.

Actions taken in the name of sustainability are liable to be worthless—indeed can be positively harmful to a company's brand and the bottom line—if the underlying principles aren't demonstrably applied to day-to-day decision-making (remember what we talked about on page 13? Sustainability isn't about PR; it's about CULTURE!).

A company's commitment to sustainability should be self-evident in the very products and services it provides, and in the manner in which it conducts its daily business.

Sustainable brands never engage in greenwash. They supercharge their sense of meaning and purpose by integrating and serving those concerns that are most relevant to their sphere of influence.

Amply illustrated by the case of BP, as long as old-fashioned notions of CSR exist as a sort of self-contained box for all the nice stuff, it will always be possible for the noblest of promises and commitments to co-exist with fundamentally unsustainable behaviours—with potentially disastrous consequences for the company concerned.

Beyond the thin veneer of charitable giving, cause-related marketing and so on, your commitment to sustainability should be self-evident in the VERY PRODUCTS AND SERVICES YOU PROVIDE, and the manner in which you conduct your daily business. Or, to use the more eloquent words of Jonathon Porritt, "ALL ACTIONS taken by a company to enhance its own commercial success should SIMULTANEOUSLY generate benefits for society, over and above those that come directly through the use of that company's products and services."

THAT'S what it means to create SHARED VALUE, and all this leads to the THIRD PRINCIPLE for building sustainable brands. Sustainable brands NEVER ENGAGE IN GREENWASH. They supercharge their sense of meaning and purpose (and hence their value) by integrating and serving those concerns that are MOST RELEVANT to their sphere of influence.

What's material to a business will vary from industry to industry, but will always revolve around its core purpose.

WHAT DOES THAT MEAN FOR MY ORGANISATION?

A few years back, a friend of mine was waxing lyrical about his international investment bank's flagship scheme to promote clean water and sustainable water use. A noble endeavour, no doubt. "Just one question," I said. "What the hell has that got to do with responsible banking?"

What's material to a bank relates to its core business—THE SUPPLY OF CAPITAL. Who am I lending money to? Can they afford to pay me back? To what use is that money going to be put? What sort of return am I expecting, and how quickly? What are the likely social and environmental consequences? In essence, what constitutes a SUSTAINABLE INVESTMENT?

In short, they're the really BIG QUESTIONS—the ones that, had banks bothered to ask them, might have made them think twice about investing in the American sub-prime market. Yours, of course, will be different, but they'll similarly go to the heart of your CORE PURPOSE as a business.

ONE PRINCIPLE, TWO DIMENSIONS

Just to go a little bit deeper, materiality is really there to be explored along TWO critical lines. The first is COMPANY-BASED materiality—that's to say what are the most prominent social and environmental impacts (both positive and

There are two sides to materiality—the social and environmental impact of what you do, and the issues that people most care about in the markets in which you operate.

negative) of your activities as a company. At a minimum, sustainability strategy should be focused on addressing impacts directly related to your sphere of operations (as described above). Better yet, sustainability should be a FUNDAMENTAL DESIGN VALUE underpinning business strategy and culture, such that your CORE PRODUCTS AND SERVICES are geared towards creating value both for the business AND for society in ONE AND THE SAME ACT.

The second dimension is MARKET-BASED materiality— i.e. what your customers most care about. That goal of creating shared value should also see efforts focused on making a positive impact on the issues and concerns considered of greatest importance to society IN THE SPECIFIC MARKETS IN WHICH YOU OPERATE.

ASKING THE RIGHT QUESTION

Really understanding these two dimensions of materiality— especially the latter—is key to creating value through action on sustainability. Imagine a mobile phone operator, for example— one based in the Middle East, where the extraordinary prevalence of chronic diseases like asthma, diabetes and coronary heart disease is a major concern for society.

Properly exploring materiality—especially the market-based dimension—can create short-term value by unlocking ideas for new products and services.

Now imagine that, instead of starting from an old-world CSR mindset and lobbing a big wedge of cash at a healthcare charity, you ask yourself a different—and much more material—kind of question. How might we unleash the power of mobile devices and applications to actually IMPROVE ACCESS TO— AND DELIVERY OF—HEALTHCARE SERVICES?

What might that look like?

Easier access to health and fitness advice? Medical consultations via video conferencing, so people in remote communities don't have to travel for days to see a doctor in the big city? Medical information being sent on by the emergency services, en route to hospital, to help surgical team prepare? Health centres using mobile applications to monitor and manage drug inventories, and dispense drugs more accurately? Telemedicine services, enabling people to track key health indicators—blood pressure, blood sugar, lung function etc.—so that they can self-manage chronic conditions and improve their quality of life?

The list goes on and on—all examples of how it's perfectly possible to create SHARED VALUE and supercharge your brand's sense of meaning and purpose by directing your core capabilities towards delivering social progress.

The precise meaning of sustainability to any given organisation is context specific. The first step in any process of strategy formulation should be to ask, "What does sustainability mean to us?"

Of course, the real mind-bender in all of this is that creating this kind of value in the short-term is actually dependent on adopting a much more LONG-TERM ORIENTATION—a different kind of mindset that views sustainability not as a leading measure of activity (at arm's length from core business), but as a LAGGING MEASURE of the cumulative, long-term impact of EVERYTHING YOU DO.

WHY NO TWO STRATEGIES WILL EVER BE THE SAME

The two dimensions of materially dictate the consideration of a combination of factors that will always vary from business to business and market to market. Whilst the basic principle remains constant, its embodiment in strategy and execution is NECESSARILY DIFFERENT in each case. Much to the chagrin of people who'd prefer you to just pull down a nice, neat cookbook solution from the shelf labelled 'Best Practice', the fact is that NO TWO STRATEGIES WILL EVER BE IDENTICAL.

In summary, the FOURTH PRINCIPLE for building sustainable brands states that the precise meaning of sustainability to any given organisation is CONTEXT SPECIFIC, based on the nature of its activities and the markets in which it operates. Because of that, the first step in any process of strategy formulation should be to figure out, "What does sustainability mean to us?"

A credible commitment to sustainability can only be built from the inside out.

BUILDING CREDIBILITY FROM THE INSIDE OUT

When it comes to action on sustainability, things are generally broken down into four key areas of activity.

→ WORKPLACE – Essentially the EMPLOYER BRAND space. How does your core purpose translate into the deal on offer for current and prospective employees? (A subject, by the way, that's worthy of an entire 55-minute guide all to itself—**BRAND AND TALENT**)

→ MARKETPLACE – How you manage relationships with customers and suppliers along the value chain, including to what extent you lead THEIR behaviours on sustainability.

→ COMMUNITY – How what you do, and how you do it, makes a positive contribution to society in the communities in which you operate.

→ ENVIRONMENT – How what you do, and how you do it, protects, conserves and (ideally) restores natural resources, and addresses the issue of climate change.

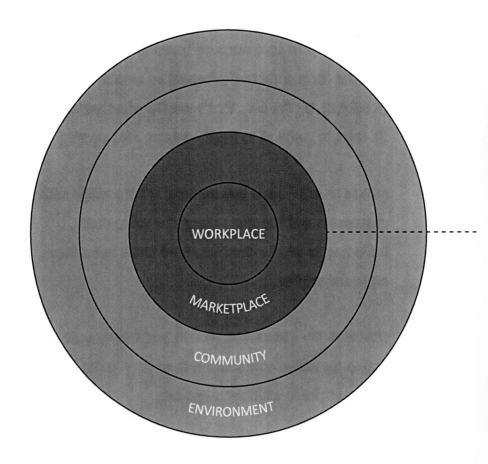

WORKPLACE

MARKETPLACE

COMMUNITY

ENVIRONMENT

A CREDIBLE COMMITMENT TO
SUSTAINABILITY CAN ONLY BE
BUILT FROM THE INSIDE OUT

Whole Foods' commitment to sustainability isn't just built on stocking natural, organic products. It's systemic, and it starts with the way they treat their own people.

Often, these are represented as a set of interconnected jigsaw pieces, each given equal weight. A much more helpful way of looking at it, though, is as a series of concentric circles, with WORKPLACE at the centre, radiating out to ENVIRONMENT.

Why? Because credibility depends on working FROM THE INSIDE OUT. Until you can demonstrate how sustainable thinking is embedded in your own organisation and along the value chain, what licence do you have to talk about anything else?

THAT WORD AUTHENTICITY AGAIN

Remember what we talked about in chapter 6—how the authenticity of a brand stems from the PROPER BRANDING OF INTERNAL CULTURE? Well, this is no different.

Take Whole Foods for example. If you think their sustainability credentials begin and end with stocking natural, organic products in their stores then think again. Scratch beneath the surface, as Gary Hamel does in **THE FUTURE OF MANAGEMENT**, and you'll find that their commitment to COMMUNITY goes way deeper than that, and it starts with the way it treats its own people. Consider, for example, the level of autonomy granted to staff to actually choose what to stock in their store. Consider their peer-based selection process that puts hiring decisions in the hands of those

Leapfrogging straight to community and environmental investments is only likely to label efforts as tactical and a bolt-on.

who'll be most affected by them. And perhaps most strikingly of all, consider a salary differential of just 19:1 between the highest paid and the company average—that versus a ratio of over 400:1 in your average Fortune 500 company (and presumably rather higher at your average investment bank!).

Even leaving aside these issues of culture and organisational design, what business does a bank have—and what value can it expect to create—talking about sustainable water use if it hasn't first dealt with the infinitely more material issue of RESPONSIBLE LENDING? (Even beyond that, there are much more relevant community concerns to a bank's core business, such as the impact of debt on society.)

What this should help to illustrate is the FIFTH PRINCIPLE for building sustainable brands. A credible commitment to sustainability starts with embedding it in CORE BUSINESS OPERATIONS, and THROUGHOUT THE VALUE CYCLE. Leapfrogging straight to community and environmental investments is only likely to label efforts as tactical and a bolt-on.

Whilst many leading corporations have sought to ride the sustainability wave, very few have succeeded in establishing sustainability as a meaningful source of advantage.

7. WHAT IT TAKES TO BE DIFFERENT

SURFING THE SUSTAINABILITY WAVE

In his excellent book, ZAG, Marty Neumeier talks about the importance of riding waves in creating powerful, charismatic brands—harnessing trends to generate a sense of raw, youthful energy. There can be few bigger waves right now than sustainability. Yet, whilst many leading corporations have sought to ride that wave, few have succeeded in establishing a credible claim to market leadership.

To help diagnose why, it's time to unleash the CR CONTINUUM—a simple framework that unpacks the transition from CR 1.0 to CR 2.0 into more bite-size steps and enables you to visualise where an organisation's strategy positions it in the broader scheme of things.

What's really important to notice is the motivation driving behaviour at each stage, and where responsibility for the agenda typically sits within the organisation.

This is the substance behind the spin. It's key because, whilst many organisations like to big themselves up as champions of sustainability, few have any real understanding of what it takes to occupy that space with any credibility.

THE CR CONTINUUM FRAMEWORK IS A GREAT WAY OF DETECTING AND AVOIDING GREENWASH

LEVEL ONE
Achieving compliance

LEVEL TWO
Window dressing

MOTIVATION
Avoiding negative
consequences of
non-compliance

APPROACH
Driven by legal.
Doing the minimum
necessary to maintain
licence to operate

LONGEVITY
Initiatives stop if
legal requirements
change or fall away

MOTIVATION
Benefits to internal
and public image

APPROACH
Driven by PR. Specific
initiatives designed
to protect and
enhance reputation

LONGEVITY
Initiatives stop if
public or employee
interest change
or fall away

LEVEL THREE
Being less bad

LEVEL FOUR
A force for good

LEVEL FIVE
Global thought leader

MOTIVATION
Minimising negative impacts of existing business model

APPROACH
Owned by CR department. Search for balance between economic, ethical and ecological demands (triple bottom line)

LONGEVITY
May survive loss of interest, provided business case remains sound

MOTIVATION
Identifying opportunities for disruptive innovation and shared value creation

APPROACH
Owned by everyone. Sustainability adopted as fundemental design value, integral to culture and strategy (triple top line)

LONGEVITY
Focus only modifies to align with new paradigms

MOTIVATION
Sustainability seen as global imperative

APPROACH
Owned by everyone. Looking beyond own business to engage others in moving up the Continuum

LONGEVITY
Limited only by other organisations' commitment to development

People have turned their BS detectors up to eleven. Your claims are being subjected to unprecedented scrutiny, and if they don't stack up, you'll end up doing your brand more harm than good. (Just ask Tony Hayward of BP!)

Where most organisations go wrong is that their rhetoric simply doesn't match the reality. Feeling under pressure to communicate a clear stance on ethical and environmental issues, they succumb to the temptation of the quick fix.

Ambitious targets and headline-grabbing initiatives are launched, accompanied by all the usual PR bull and the CEO's big speech about 'leading the way'. Trouble is, whilst the language might position them at Level Four or Five on the CR CONTINUUM, more often than not, the reality is firmly rooted at Level Two or Three, and that's a sure-fire recipe for accusations of greenwash.

Remembering the changes described earlier in chapter 5, companies need to wake up and smell the fairtrade coffee. Their claims are being subjected to UNPRECEDENTED LEVELS OF SCRUTINY. The authenticity gap will be found out, and any claim that doesn't stand up to closer examination will end up doing the brand more harm than good.

Many more companies will learn the hard way that it's better to DO THEN SAY when it comes to sustainability, and that brings us to the SIXTH PRINCIPLE for building sustainable brands—one exemplified by sustainability thought leaders like Interface and Marks & Spencer. A credible commitment to sustainability is built on ACHIEVEMENT, not statements of intent.

Old-world CSR is meaningless as a source of advantage. It's nothing more than a hygiene factor.

Sustainable brands illustrate progress towards a clear, long-term vision, backed up by MEANINGFUL PROOF POINTS.

If you haven't got that far yet, then go back to the principles of awareness, responsiveness and materiality. Communicate what you're doing to understand your impacts on society and the environment. Publish your audit. Demonstrate your commitment to an open dialogue with friends and critics about the next steps.

In short, the moral of the story is MORE HASTE, LESS SPEED. Take the time to do things properly. There are plenty of ways to generate goodwill without rushing into superficial, big budget initiatives that'll just end up being counterproductive.

LOOKING BEYOND THE TRIPLE BOTTOM LINE

As every man and his dog looks to stake his ethical and ecological credentials, the simple truth is that old-world CSR is meaningless as a source of advantage. It's just a HYGIENE FACTOR.

Why? Because it's only interested in making the existing business model appear LESS BAD. The 'giving something back' mindset pays little or no heed to WHAT YOU TAKE IN THE FIRST PLACE. This leaves the underlying model fundamentally unchanged, offering little or no ground for differentiation

Radical differentiation and competitive advantage depend on new business models that emphasise doing good, not just shoring up the old model by making it less bad.

beyond subjective arguments over the sincerity of companies' commitments and who's 'doing it better' (arguments that are always going to be very difficult and expensive to try and win).

The key to being different—REALLY DIFFERENT—is to make the transition from Level Three to Level Four on the CR CONTINUUM. This is where companies begin to ask a completely different kind of question—not, "What can I do to shore up the old order?" but, "WHAT CAN I DO TO SHAPE A NEW ONE?"

This is what truly distinguishes market leading, sustainable brands—whether that's industrial behemoths like Interface completely transforming its petrochemical intensive business in pursuit of ZERO IMPACT ON THE ENVIRONMENT; whether it's a comparative new kid on the block like performance clothing brand, Icebreaker, taking inspiration from Mother Nature to create A TOTALLY NEW MARKET SEGMENT and stand out from the synthetic competition; or whether its a regional brewer in the idyllic Suffolk countryside, Adnams, building its new distribution centre with a sedum roof (and a host of other ground-breaking features), not only avoiding inflicting the usual eyesore on locals, but also contributing to a marketing first—THE UK'S FIRST EVER CARBON NEUTRAL BEER!

RADICAL DIFFERENTIATION ONLY COMES
WHEN SUSTAINABILITY IS ADOPTED
AS A FUNDAMENTAL DESIGN VALUE

LEVEL ONE
Achieving compliance

LEVEL TWO
Window dressing

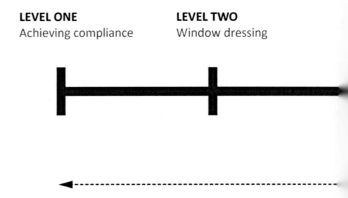

CR 1.0
Old-world CSR has already
become nothing more than
a hygiene factor

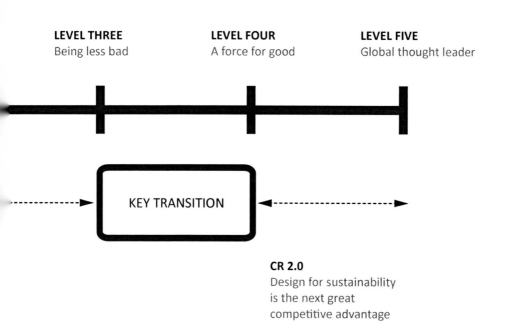

LEVEL THREE
Being less bad

LEVEL FOUR
A force for good

LEVEL FIVE
Global thought leader

KEY TRANSITION

CR 2.0
Design for sustainability
is the next great
competitive advantage

Imagine a future in which you were legally obliged to take back every product you ever made. How might that change your behaviour?

8. DESIGN FOR SUSTAINABILITY

What the previous chapter boils down to is our SEVENTH AND FINAL PRINCIPLE for building sustainable brands. BEING LESS BAD IS NOT THE SAME AS BEING GOOD. Sustainability is only a meaningful and lasting source of competitive advantage when adopted as a FUNDAMENTAL DESIGN VALUE that challenges existing practices and paves the way for DISRUPTIVE INNOVATION.

As a starting point, consider this brilliant question posed by Marty Neumeier in **THE DESIGNFUL COMPANY**.

→   Imagine a future in which you were legally obliged to TAKE BACK EVERY PRODUCT YOU EVER MADE. How might that change your behaviour?

Personally, I think that's genius, not least as it instantly frames sustainability as a matter of CORE BUSINESS AND CULTURE, rather than old-fashioned, arm's-length philanthropy. What makes me chuckle about it, though, is that it's a question verging on the rhetorical. It doesn't take a brain the size of a planet to figure out the kinds of things that might entail—just the cojones to ditch most of what you learned in B-school and take the path less travelled.

'Waste equals food' is a fundamental law of nature, and a key principle of design for sustainability.

For a more comprehensive picture of what it means to design for sustainability, it's well worth checking out THE LIVING PRINCIPLES—a terrific framework inspired by Adam Werbach's book, **STRATEGY FOR SUSTAINABILITY**. For now, though, let's focus on two aspects that, for me, offer the most promising avenues for business transformation.

ELIMINATING THE VERY CONCEPT OF WASTE

Perhaps the single most important design principle—and the one that speaks loudest to the inner operational efficiency geek in every manager—is the goal of driving out waste. Not reducing waste, mind you, but ELIMINATING IT AS A CONCEPT.

Waste doesn't exist in the natural world. The waste from one part of the system simply becomes food for another, and that's the blueprint. In a world of diminishing resources and rocketing oil prices, CHEAP CAN NO LONGER GO HAND-IN-HAND WITH DISPOSABLE. Natural assets need to be made to sweat infinitely harder by the use of CRADLE TO CRADLE DESIGN— products, packaging and indeed entire business models that are built around smart choices about material inputs and how these can be given LIFE BEYOND LIFE by maintaining them in a CLOSED LOOP.

In a world of diminishing resources, the market leading businesses of tomorrow will be the ones that succeed in replacing value chains with value cycles.

In **THE NEW CAPITALIST MANIFESTO**, Umair Haque neatly describes the mindset shift as a move from value chains to VALUE CYCLES—from economies of scale to ECONOMIES OF CYCLE, whereby each cycle not only reduces the average cost of materials, but also effectively amortises and offsets the fixed costs of production.

Sounds great, right? And these are the kinds of questions you need to ask yourself:

→ MATERIAL INPUTS – How might you redesign products and processes to reduce the amount and types of materials used? Do you have a means to assess whether those inputs are cyclable so that material waste is no longer waste, but the food for another process? Could your raw materials come from someone else's waste (or your waste become someone else's raw material)?

→ LONGEVITY AND MODULARITY – What's the expected lifespan of your product? How easily can it be repaired, updated or put to alternative use? How easily can it be disassembled, and waste streams separated to aid their repurposing and reuse?

After 3.8 billion years of evolution, there probably isn't a single design challenge that hasn't already been efficiently and elegantly solved in the natural world.

→ CLOSING THE LOOP – How can you make use of reverse logistics to reclaim discarded outputs and turn them into new inputs? How close are the points of production and consumption? Can these distances be shortened to further increase the efficiency of your value cycle?

MOTHER NATURE—THE GREAT INNOVATOR

WASTE EQUALS FOOD is by no means the only thing we can learn from Mother Nature. After 3.8 billion years of evolution, there probably isn't a single design challenge that hasn't already been efficiently and elegantly solved in the natural world, and that's the basic premise underlying BIOMIMICRY— the burgeoning field of nature-inspired innovation popularised by the work of Janine Benyus. Her **ASK NATURE** online database just goes to show the rich seam of innovative ideas that is there to be mined, if we only take time to look. Here are just three...

→ The merino wool fibre is a remarkable thing, helping sheep in the New Zealand alps to stay warm in winter and cool in summer. A perfect, sustainable alternative, then, to synthetic outdoor performance clothing—an epiphany upon which Jeremy Moon, CEO of Icebreaker, has successfully built a $multi-million business.

As long as customers are asked to pay a substantial premium for more socially responsible and eco-friendly performance, products and services will only ever appeal to a well-to-do niche.

→ Sharklet™ mimics the microbe-resistant properties of sharkskin. A distinct nano-scale pattern—put into adhesive-backed film and manufactured into medical devices—inhibits bacteria growth without the need for harsh chemicals and biocides that have made bacteria stronger and contributed to the rise in antibiotic-resistant superbugs like MRSA.

→ Inspired by the fog-gathering technique of the Namib desert beetle, the Dew Bank Bottle is being designed to harvest water from the air, where fresh drinking water is scarce. Resembling the beetle's body, the domed steel structure is placed outside at night. In the morning, when the surrounding air begins to warm, water droplets condense and are channelled down ridges in the surface to collect in an enclosed chamber for drinking water. (Genius!)

BEYOND THE WORLD OF TRADE-OFFS

For too long, the great Achilles' heel of green marketing has been a value proposition that demands customers pay a premium for more socially responsible and/or more eco-friendly performance. In that world, sustainable products and services

Generating mass market appeal requires sustainable products to at least match (and preferably outperform) their unsustainable rivals across all dimensions of value. Only then can their eco-credentials stand out as a genuine differentiator.

will only ever appeal to a well-to-do niche who are prepared to make such a trade-off.

I focus on the two strands above—the re-imagining of business systems as value cycles and nature-inspired innovation—for good reason, and that's because they move us into completely different territory, recasting the value disciplines of operational excellence and product leadership for the 21st century.

The beauty of re-imagining businesses as value cycles, such as Interface is doing with its ReEntry service, and Patagonia with Common Threads, is that you eventually end up with a totally different and infinitely more compelling value proposition—superior sustainable performance at a cost that is EQUIVALENT TO OR EVEN LOWER THAN the unsustainable alternative.

Similarly, the beauty of nature-inspired innovation, is that it presents the opportunity develop sustainable products and services that actually OUTPERFORM their unsustainable rivals. Icebreaker gear doesn't command a premium price point just because it's 'green'. It does so because it's a BETTER PRODUCT. It insulates every bit as well as the synthetic competition, but with the added advantage that it feels great against your skin and it doesn't leave you humming like a nuclear reactor when you take it off after a run!

If the words brand, design and sustainability don't already loom large in your boardroom, then they should. They are increasingly important lenses through which to view innovation, value creation and business transformation.

9. IS YOUR BUSINESS FIT FOR PURPOSE?

On that note, it's probably about time we wrapped things up—after all, our 55 minutes must be running out by now. Let's close with a quick elevator pitch to round up the basic argument of this book. It runs something like this...

THE PITCH

BRAND. DESIGN. SUSTAINABILITY. If these words don't already loom large in the lexicon of your boardroom, then they should. Given the values shift we are already seeing as a result of the global financial crisis, they are increasingly important lenses through which to view INNOVATION, VALUE CREATION and BUSINESS TRANSFORMATION.

Why? Because the consequences of THIN VALUE— of profit decoupled from the people and resources impacted by its generation—have been exposed like never before in our lifetime. In order to REBUILD CREDIBILITY, DEMONSTRATE RELEVANCE and ACHIEVE LASTING AND MEANINGFUL DIFFERENTIATION, the big challenge facing corporations today is how to deliver THICKER VALUE.

The big challenge facing corporations today is how to deliver thicker value—building a value proposition that is purpose-driven, beneficial to society, and self-evident in everything you do.

→ THICK VALUE means uniting all stakeholders around a CLEAR SENSE OF PURPOSE. More than ever before, the organisation that wants to achieve long-term success must earth itself in a sure sense of why it exists, what it stands for, and why it matters. And that purpose must be seen to guide congruent actions and behaviours. That's STRATEGIC BRANDING.

→ THICK VALUE means connecting brand and business strategy to a HIGHER SOCIAL PURPOSE—not taking 'business as usual' for granted and merely minimising the unfortunate side effects, but rather seeking to MAXIMISE THE PRIMARY EFFECTS of what you do. CREATING SHARED VALUE by directing core competencies towards delivering social progress is what real sustainability is all about, and (according to the likes of Michael Porter) it's the next great competitive advantage.

→ THICK VALUE means being AUTHENTIC—ensuring that this strategic intent is SELF-EVIDENT in the very products and services you provide, how you organise yourself, and how you conduct your daily business. In other words, it has to be BAKED INTO EVERYTHING YOU DO—BY DESIGN.

Like Pascal's Wager, whether or not you agree with the contents of this book, it still makes logical sense to act as if you do.

THE HEDGE

If all of this seems a bit rich—or maybe you're inclined to buy into it, but you're waiting for more definitive proof before you commit to action—think about it this way.

If you make the leap and open your mind to the possibilities, and this whole thesis is wrong, what have you really lost? If climate change was revealed to be a complete myth tomorrow, would it still make sense to pursue energy efficiency and more renewable energy sources?

YOU BET IT WOULD!

Conversely, if you choose to ignore the signs, and this thesis is right, by the time your longed-for definitive proof arrives, the chances are YOU'LL ALREADY HAVE BEEN OUTCOMPETED. (As those smart cookies over at Google say, better to disrupt yourself than to wait for someone else to come along and do it for you!)

Ultimately, it's a bit like PASCAL'S WAGER.

Whether or not you truly believe in any of this sustainability stuff is actually immaterial. It still makes logical sense to act as if you do—BECAUSE THE CONSEQUENCE OF BETTING THE WRONG WAY COULD BE OBSOLESCENCE!

10. TAKE-HOME LESSONS

It's been a bit of a whirlwind tour so—in case you missed them—here's a quick recap on the SEVEN PRINCIPLES for building sustainable brands.

→ For a brand to survive and prosper over the long-term, it must be distinctive and memorable but, above all, IT MUST BE TRUE. Particularly for corporate and service brands, authenticity rests on THE PROPER BRANDING OF INTERNAL CULTURE.

→ Sustainability is too pervasive to be managed along narrow, functional lines. It is the responsibility of EVERYONE IN THE ORGANISATION and requires an INTERDISCIPLINARY APPROACH to strategy and communications.

→ Sustainable brands NEVER ENGAGE IN GREENWASH. They supercharge their sense of meaning and purpose (and hence their value) by integrating and serving those concerns that are MOST RELEVANT TO THEIR SPHERE OF INFLUENCE.

→ The precise meaning of sustainability to any given organisation is CONTEXT SPECIFIC, based on the nature of its activities and the markets in which it operates. Because of that, the first step in any process of strategy formulation should be to ask, "What does sustainability mean to us?"

→ A credible commitment to sustainability starts with embedding it in CORE BUSINESS OPERATIONS, and THROUGHOUT THE VALUE CYCLE. Leapfrogging straight to community and environmental investments is only likely to label efforts as tactical and a bolt-on.

→ A credible commitment to sustainability is built on ACHIEVEMENT, NOT STATEMENTS OF INTENT. Sustainable brands emphasise progress towards a CLEAR, LONG-TERM VISION, backed up by MEANINGFUL PROOF POINTS.

→ BEING LESS BAD IS NOT THE SAME AS BEING GOOD. Sustainability is only a meaningful and lasting source of competitive advantage when adopted as a FUNDAMENTAL DESIGN VALUE that challenges existing practices and paves the way for DISRUPTIVE INNOVATION.

11. BRAND AND SUSTAINABILITY GLOSSARY

When it comes to brand and sustainability, a lot of terms get bandied around by a lot of people in a lot of different ways. Just to be clear, here's what I mean when I say...

AUTHENTICITY – undisputed credibility; the quality of being genuine. (The Holy Grail of sustainable brands.)

BIOMIMICRY – using the natural world—its models, systems, processes and elements—as inspiration for innovation.

BRAND – a set of tacit assumptions and preconscious beliefs that other people hold about your organisation and how it operates. It's what they say it is, not you.

CLOSED LOOP – a sustainable system of production, including reverse logistics, in which materials may be brought 'back to life' as new products, rather than discarded as waste.

CORPORATE CITIZENSHIP – term referring specifically to an organisation's philanthropic and charitable activities. Often (wrongly) used as used as an alternative to CORPORATE RESPONSIBILITY or SUSTAINABILITY (see below).

CORPORATE RESPONSIBILITY (CR) – alternative to CSR (see below) that, in dropping the 'S', used to be considered more appropriate for describing an organisation's management of the full range of its social and environmental impacts. Still firmly rooted in a 'less bad' mindset, though, and a far cry from new-world SUSTAINABILITY (see below).

CORPORATE SOCIAL RESPONSIBILITY (CSR) – defunct term, long since abandoned by thought leaders as both inaccurate (inferring the exclusion of environmental concerns) and tainted by association with GREENWASH (see below).

CR 1.0 – shorthand denoting the first generation of corporate responsibility strategy and communications, typified by PR driven approaches and old-fashioned corporate philanthropy. CR is seen as a separate agenda, rather than an integral part of strategy and culture.

CR 2.0 – shorthand denoting the new generation of sustainability strategy and communications, which emphasises the use of sustainability as a fundamental design value to interrogate, challenge and transform existing practices. Sustainability is seen as a key strategic driver of innovation and value creation.

CRADLE TO CRADLE – a metaphor to symbolise the cyclical alternative to our hitherto linear 'take, make, waste' model of manufacturing and consumption. See also VALUE CYCLE.

CULTURE – basic assumptions about an organisation and the way it functions, typically shaped by shared values and learning experiences ('The way we do things around here').

CUSTOMER INTIMACY – one of three VALUE DISCIPLINES (see below), typified by the cultivation of deep, one-to-one relationships. Competitive advantage comes from offering the best total solution, tailored to the customer's specific circumstances and requirements.

DESIGN – the conscious and intuitive effort by which we change existing situations into preferred ones.

DISRUPTIVE INNOVATION – radical innovation that defines new market space and ultimately supersedes incumbent services and technologies.

GREENWASH – superficial or disingenuous attempts to present companies, products or services as environmentally friendly; anything that falls into the category of 'CR as PR'.

HYGIENE FACTOR – something that is notable and important only when it is lacking.

LICENCE TO OPERATE – the freedom to carry out one's business. Increasingly referred to not only in the context of legally granted permission, but also of gaining broader social acceptance.

MATERIALITY – the extent to which an company's actions on sustainability are relevant to its sphere of operations, and important to stakeholders in its chosen markets.

OPERATIONAL EXCELLENCE – another of the three VALUE DISCIPLINES (see below), typified by incredibly streamlined operations and superb execution. Competitive advantage is derived by offering customers dependable quality at low prices.

PRODUCT LEADERSHIP – a third VALUE DISCIPLINE (see below), typified by excellence in innovation and brand marketing. Competitive advantage comes from perpetually pushing the boundaries of design and product performance.

PURPOSE – the reason your business exists (beyond making money). Why should your people feel inspired to get out of bed in the morning? If you ceased to exist tomorrow, why should anyone care?

SHARED VALUE – where value for a business and value for society is created in one and the same act, by virtue of connecting core strategy to social progress.

SIMPLICITY – the supreme excellence, according to Henry Wadsworth Longfellow. AUTHENTICITY and TRANSPARENCY are impossible without it.

SUSTAINABILITY – a perspective on brand and business strategy that inextricably links long-term business success with serving a higher social purpose. In a game of word association, sustainability should spark the word 'longevity' before it does the word 'green'.

THICK VALUE – see SHARED VALUE above.

THIN VALUE – profits decoupled from the people and resources impacted by their generation, and which are therefore both unsustainable and meaningless in terms of the betterment of society.

TRANSPARENCY – the process of making it simple for stakeholders to understand and fairly interpret an organisation's decisions and conduct. (Note: it has nothing to with the volume of information made available; it's about the usefulness of that information in forming reasonable judgements.)

TRIPLE BOTTOM LINE – a broader means of measuring corporate performance, seeking to balance the goal of economic growth with concerns for environmental protection and social equity.

TRIPLE TOP LINE – a perspective that draws upon BIOMIMICRY (see above) to design products and systems that are intrinsically beneficial to society and whose constituent materials can be continually reclaimed and 'reborn' as new products.

VALUE CYCLE – an alternative perspective on the traditional value chain; emphasises the addition of a 'back to life' cycle, whereby materials may be re-used, reducing their average cost and amortising the fixed costs of production.

VALUE DISCIPLINES – term referring to Michael Treacy and Fred Wiersema's theory on how companies can build sustainable competitive advantage. The central premise: businesses cannot seek to be all things to all people; they must choose to excel in a specific dimension of value (either OPERATIONAL EXCELLENCE, PRODUCT LEADERSHIP or CUSTOMER INTIMACY – see above) and structure themselves accordingly.

12. AFTERWORD

This book is only ever going to be a starting point. Whether you violently agree or disagree with its contents, I hope it will have inspired you to want to learn more. If it has, then—as has become customary in the 55-minute guide series—here's a list of further reading you may find useful.

If you read no other book on this list, make it Ray C. Anderson's CONFESSIONS OF A RADICAL INDUSTRIALIST. A one-line dedication to Ray cannot possibly do justice to the influence that the Interface story has had on me and, when you read it, you'll understand why. It's one thing for the likes of Icebreaker to build sustainability into their business from the off; it's quite another to completely reinvent an established $billion corporation—one built on converting petrochemicals into textiles to boot.

The reason the story is so important is simple. As Ray himself said in a fabulous TED Talk, if Interface can transform itself into a truly sustainable enterprise, then it follows that ANY business can. (There, the gauntlet has been laid down!)

I hope you've enjoyed this quick jaunt round the world of brand and sustainability, and look forward to continuing the conversation with you on the LIVE LONG AND PROSPER blog.

THE BIG IDEA – ROBERT JONES

BIOMIMICRY – JANINE BENYUS

BRAND-DRIVEN INNOVATION – ERIK ROSCAM ABBING

THE BRAND GAP, ZAG, THE DESIGNFUL COMPANY – MARTY NEUMEIER

BUILT TO LAST – JIM COLLINS & JERRY PORRAS

CAPITALISM AS IF THE WORLD MATTERS – JONATHON PORRITT

CHANGE BY DESIGN – TIM BROWN

CONFESSIONS OF A RADICAL INDUSTRIALIST – RAY C. ANDERSON

CRADLE TO CRADLE – BILL MCDONOUGH & MICHAEL BRAUNGART

THE DESIGN OF BUSINESS, THE OPPOSABLE MIND – ROGER MARTIN

THE DISCIPLINE OF MARKET LEADERS – MICHAEL TREACY & FRED WIERSEMA

DRIVE – DAN PINK

THE ECOLOGY OF COMMERCE – PAUL HAWKEN

EMERGENCE, WHERE GOOD IDEAS COME FROM – STEVEN JOHNSON

THE FUTURE OF MANAGEMENT – GARY HAMEL

THE FUTURE OF THE FUTURE – RICHARD SEYMOUR

GOOD BUSINESS – STEVE HILTON & GILES GIBBONS

LET MY PEOPLE GO SURFING – YVON CHOUINARD

THE NEW CAPITALIST MANIFESTO – UMAIR HAQUE

PREDICTABLY IRRATIONAL – DAN ARIELY

STRATEGY FOR SUSTAINABILITY – ADAM WERBACH

SWITCH – CHIP & DAN HEATH

THE TIPPING POINT – MALCOLM GLADWELL

ASK NATURE – WWW.ASKNATURE.ORG

FORCE FOR GOOD – WWW.FORCEFORGOOD.COM

ICEBREAKER – WWW.ICEBREAKER.COM

INTERFACE – WWW.INTERFACEGLOBAL.COM

THE LIVING PRINCIPLES – WWW.LIVINGPINCIPLES.ORG

MARKS & SPENCER – PLANA.MARKSANDSPENCER.COM/ABOUT

THE MIX – WWW.MANAGEMENTEXCHANGE.COM

TED TALKS – WWW.TED.COM/THEMES/A_GREENER_FUTURE.HTML

ABOUT THE AUTHOR

Management consultant. Sustainability advocate. Brand strategist. MBA graduate. Integrative thinker. Linguist. Author. Storyteller. Armchair anthropologist. Family man. Rugby nut. Germanophile. Amateur chef. Giant.

Depending on whom you ask, DAN GRAY is a lot of things. While that might seem a little messy to some, he insists there's method to the madness—all fuelled by a preoccupation with how brand, sustainability and design thinking can be woven together to help organisations create THICKER VALUE.

As a consultant, he's worked with several leading brand and design agencies—including Publicis Consultants and Seymourpowell—and has helped to win new business and deliver major projects with clients including Barclays Capital, Ernst & Young, Etisalat, KPMG, Lloyds Banking Group, Paclantic, Sainsbury's, Savills and Tetra Pak.

Besides this, maintaining his LIVE LONG AND PROSPER blog and editing other titles in the 55-minute guide series, he's also a Visiting Fellow of the Ashridge Centre for Business and Sustainability (ACBAS), an occasional contributor to forceforgood.com, and a co-founder of the CommScrum LinkedIn community.

When he's not working, he's most likely to be found mucking around with his little girl, cooking up a storm in the kitchen, or in the stands at the Madejski Stadium cheering on London Irish.

You can reach him at danmgray@yahoo.co.uk, through his blog (danmgray.wordpress.com) or via LinkedIn (www.linkedin.com/in/danmgray).

ABOUT THE BOOKS

Far too many business books start with the false premise that offering meaningful insight requires exhaustive detail. They demand a huge investment from readers to wade through all the information provided and draw out what is relevant to them.

In a rapidly changing, time-starved world, it's an approach that's getting wronger and wronger. What CEOs and other busy business people desperately need is high-level strategic insight delivered in quick, simple, easy-to-digest packages.

Co-created by DAN GRAY and KEVIN KEOHANE, that's exactly what the 55-MINUTE GUIDES are designed to do. Instead of some 300-page pseudo-academic tome, they offer fresh perspectives and must-knows on important topics that can be read from cover to cover in the course of a single morning's commute or a short plane ride.

In short, they are the antidote to most business books. A QUICK READ, not a long slog. Focused on BIG IDEAS, not technical detail. Promoting JOINED-UP THINKING, not functional bias. Written to EMPOWER THE READER, not to make the author look clever.

They're guided by the simple principle that INSIGHT GAINED PER MINUTE SPENT READING should be as high as possible. No fluff. No filler. No jargon. Just the things you REALLY need to know, written in plain English with clear and simple illustrations.

Lightning Source UK Ltd.
Milton Keynes UK
UKOW040412110713

213571UK00001B/19/P